BUILDING BLOCKS OF ANIMALS AND PLANTS

PLANT AND ANIMAL ADAPTATIONS

Written by Joseph Midthun

Illustrated by Samuel Hiti

WORLD BOOK

a Scott Fetzer company
Chicago

World Book, Inc.
180 North LaSalle Street
Suite 900
Chicago, Illinois 60601
USA

For information about other World Book publications,
visit our website at **www.worldbook.com**
or call **1-800-WORLDBK (967-5325).**
For information about sales to schools and libraries,
call 1-800-975-3250 (United States),
or 1-800-837-5365 (Canada).

Library of Congress Cataloging-in-Publication Data
for this volume has been applied for.

Building Blocks of Animals and Plants
ISBN: 978-0-7166-4616-7 (set, hc.)

Plant and Animal Adaptations
ISBN: 978-0-7166-4620-4 (hc.)

Also available as:
ISBN: 978-0-7166-4628-0 (e-book)

1st printing March 2022

WORLD BOOK STAFF
Executive Committee
President: Geoff Broderick
Vice President, Editorial: Tom Evans
Vice President, Finance: Donald D. Keller
Vice President, Marketing: Jean Lin
Vice President, International Sales:
    Eddy Kisman
Vice President, Technology: Jason Dole
Vice President, Customer Success:
    Jade Lewandowski
Director, Human Resources: Bev Ecker

Editorial
Manager, New Content: Jeff De La Rosa
Associate Manager, New Product:
    Nicholas Kilzer
Sr. Editor: Shawn Brennan
Proofreader: Nathalie Strassheim

Graphics and Design
Sr. Visual Communications Designer:
    Melanie Bender
Sr. Web Designer/Digital Media Developer:
    Matt Carrington
Coordinator, Design Development and
    Production: Brenda B. Tropinski
Book Design: Samuel Hiti

Acknowledgments:
Created by Samuel Hiti and Joseph Midthun
Art by Samuel Hiti
Additional art by David Shephard/
    The Bright Agency
Additional spot art by Shutterstock
Text by Joseph Midthun

TABLE OF CONTENTS

There is a glossary on page 39. Terms defined in the glossary
are in type **that looks like this** on their first appearance.

All living things, called **organisms,** have certain activities and needs— **characteristics**—in common.

All organisms use energy to sense and react to changes in their surroundings.

Animals move around to find food for energy.

Plants stay in one place and make their own food.

All organisms also need water and space to live.

If an organism's basic needs are met, it can grow and possibly **reproduce,** or make more of its own kind.

If these basic needs are not met, the organism will die.

FLOP

Living things meet their basic needs by interacting with their surroundings, or **environment.**

If an organism doesn't get what it needs from its environment, it doesn't just quit–

It adapts!

Adaptation is a characteristic of an organism that makes it better able to survive and reproduce in its environment.

Both plants and animals have learned to adapt to survive.

Adaptation can be as simple as moving to a new place...

Boing

...or as complex as the effects that new location can have on future generations.

plop

Adaptations develop and spread through a process called **natural selection**.

Twap

Natural selection happens when a **trait**, such as size or color, shows some **variation**, or difference.

Burp

For example, one variation of traits in moths is wing color.

Some individuals have variations that make them more likely to survive and reproduce in an environment.

Other organisms do not compete as well for food, water, and mates.

In this case, more brown moths survive because their wing color helps them go unnoticed by their **predators.**

The brown moths pass on their color trait to their offspring, creating more brown moths in the environment.

The next brown moths can go on to be successful in that environment.

Because animals and plants have adapted over time to their surroundings, there are lots of differences among living things in any environment.

This is called an **ecosystem.**

Some organisms can live in many different environments.

Sploosh

Other organisms have adapted to need specific surroundings to survive.

If you suddenly swapped a frog and a polar bear into each other's environments...

...they would most likely not survive.

All environments change. How fast environments change depends on your point of view.

To this baobab tree, it might not seem like the environment is changing much at all.

For some organisms, the changes might be beneficial.

clop clop

For others, not so much...

clop

clop

...if a living thing cannot adapt to a change in its environment, it often dies.

But those who learn to adapt are successful!

ADAPTATIONS OVER TIME

Adaptation is also the ability of organisms to adjust to changing conditions in the environment.

Humans have the ability to live in a wide range of environments.

From high mountaintops, to below sea level, your body can adapt to help you settle in that area.

Some animals, like dogs, adapt to warm weather by shedding their outermost layer of fur.

Shake Shake

Shake

Plants can adapt to changing temperatures by absorbing and storing extra water to use during dry periods.

Slurp

Many **species** develop these special features while adapting over time to slow changes in their surroundings.

Adaptations for survival allow animals to eat, to move, and to sense their environment.

Right!

Legs, wings, and fins help animals move.

Teeth and jaws help them eat.

snap

Lungs and gills help animals obtain oxygen.

Yep.

Eyes and ears help to find food and detect threats.

Human brains have adapted over time to be able to learn new skills.

Adaptations are happening all the time!

gulp

PLANT ADAPTATIONS

Many scientists think that plants developed from green **algae** that lived in fresh water a long time ago.

Changes in the environment caused the algae to adapt over many **generations**.

Eventually, algae could survive on land.

This spread of plants changed the land, providing **habitats** for many organisms.

Plants and other living things grew and adapted into many new types of organisms as they spread over the land.

When they moved on land, plant structures needed to adapt to grow upright and absorb water and nutrients from the soil.

Plants also developed a special body system for making their own food... a leaf!

Leaves use energy from sunlight, water, and a gas called carbon dioxide to make the food for the plant.

The plant can then use the food to grow or store it for later.

This process is called **photosynthesis.**

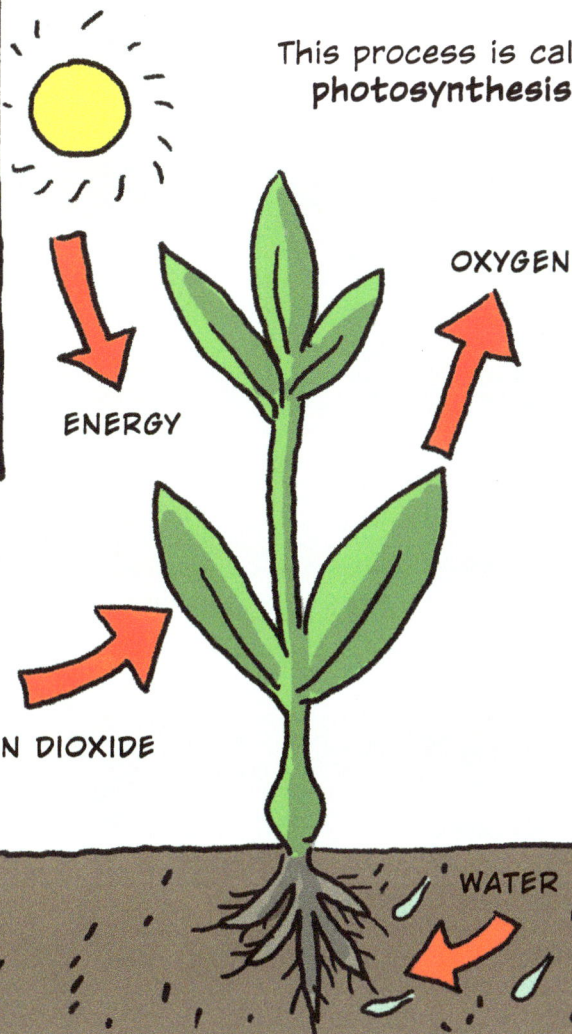

OXYGEN

ENERGY

Photosynthesis occurs in green plants, algae, and some microscopic organisms.

CARBON DIOXIDE

WATER

EATING

Animals get food by eating plants or by eating animals that eat plants.

Teeth and jaws are adaptations for bringing the food into the body.

Teeth are adapted for the particular type of food an animal eats.

Deer, giraffes, and other animals that eat plants have teeth with broad surfaces for grinding grasses and plants into small bits.

munch munch

The powerful front teeth of beavers enable these animals to cut down trees for food and shelter.

Snap

Meat-eating lions have razor-sharp, pointed teeth for biting and tearing.

A hawk has a sharp, hooked beak for piercing and ripping its prey.

A woodpecker uses its long, pointed bill to drill into the bark of trees to find insects.

Insects have jaws and movable mouthparts that act like teeth.

The jaws of grasshoppers are adapted for cutting and chewing plants.

munch munch

Mosquitoes have needle-shaped mouthparts for piercing skin and sucking blood.

Poke

How do your teeth and jaws help you eat food?

Slap

Both plants and animals have to guard against other organisms that want to eat them—

—predators.

munch munch

Some **prey** animals have adapted specialized body parts that protect them from predators.

Ribbit!

Sniff Sniff

For example, poison dart frogs have toxic skin that discourages predators from eating them.

The frog's bright skin colors warn predators that it is poisonous.

Ribbit!

Some plants have thorns that hurt animals that might try to eat them.

Other animals' outward appearance helps them blend into their natural surroundings for protection.

This adaptation is called **camouflaging.**

The fur of some small animals of northern regions turns white during the winter months to blend in with the snow.

The fur of these same animals turns brown in the summer months to help them disappear into the wooded landscape.

Some lizards also have this ability.

A chameleon's skin may be green, yellow, or tan one minute, and the next minute it may be brown, black, or even dotted or blotched!

Adapting their external appearances helps these prey animals from being spotted by a lurking predator!

17

PLANT ADAPTATIONS ON LAND

One of the most important parts in a plant's environment is **climate**—the temperature, amount of sunlight, and rainfall in an area.

Plants must have a steady supply of water.

Roots absorb moisture and **nutrients** from the soil, and then use them when making food.

Plants that grow in tropical rain forests have adapted to absorbing nutrients only when they are available.

The topsoil in tropical rain forests doesn't have many nutrients because heavy rainfall washes them away.

But, organisms like termites quickly break down fallen leaves and other plant matter, which puts nutrients back into the soil.

Plant roots then quickly absorb these nutrients, allowing for lush growth.

In dry desert environments, some cactuses, like this saguaro cactus, have roots that spread over large areas.

These cactuses store water in their fleshy stems instead of their spiky spine leaves.

Because of this leaf adaptation, cactuses have less surface area and are able to store more water in their stems for when it's needed.

Plants of the cold-climate tundra, like small shrubs and grasses, also have adapted to the dry conditions created by frozen soils.

The surfaces of their leaves are good at stopping water loss.

Tundra plants have adapted to grow in groups close to the ground. Snow can cover the plants, protecting them from strong winds that can pull their roots from the ground.

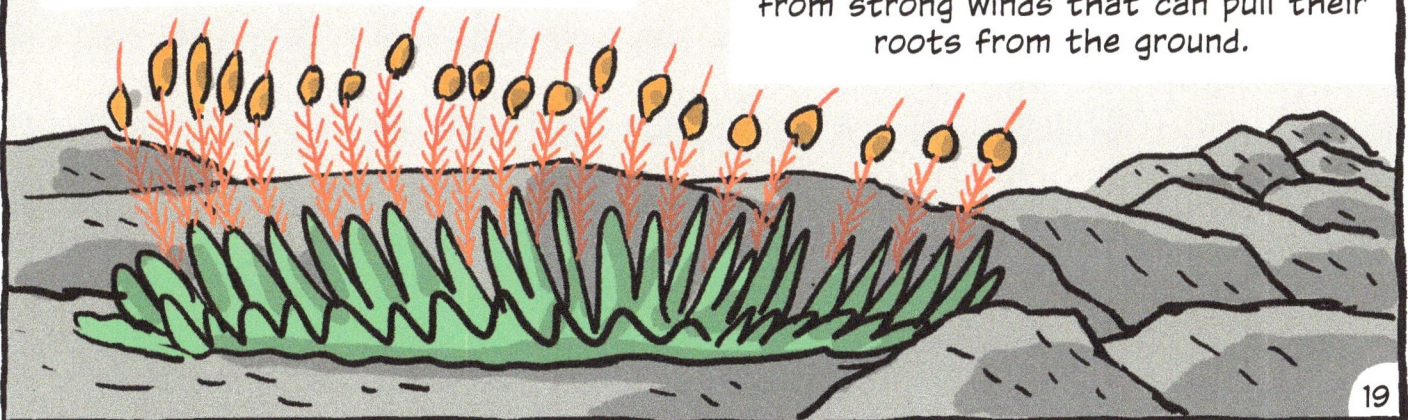

PLANT ADAPTATIONS IN WATER

Watery places have special conditions that make it difficult for many types of plants to grow, whether in fresh or salt water.

Some kinds of aquatic, or water, plants, like eelgrass, live completely underwater.

Other plants, such as duckweeds, float on the water's surface.

Still others, like the water marigold, grow only partly underwater.

Many aquatic plants have adapted to the water by keeping tiny air spaces within their stems and leaves.

The air spaces help them stand upright or stay afloat.

Mangrove forests are dense growths of mangrove trees that grow along tropical shorelines.

Mangrove plants have many adaptations to living in salty, waterlogged conditions.

These adaptations can include stilt roots that prop the plants above the water...

...bark with specialized parts that allow the plants to breathe...

...leaves that can remove extra salt...

...and seeds that float.

plop

With all of these adaptations, mangrove forests can grow large and provide a habitat for many coastal animals.

How do you sense your environment?

Most animals have adapted by developing special body parts that respond to changes in their environment.

The reactions of most animals depend on one or more of the major **senses:**

Some senses are more important to one kind of animal than to another.

hearing, sight, smell, taste, and touch.

swif

Most birds, like the great horned owl, cannot find food if they cannot see it.

A keen sense of smell helps dogs and wolves to find food, follow trails, and recognize danger.

sniff sniff

Taste is very important to insects. Some butterflies can taste the sweetness of nectar with their feet.

And plants might be the most sensitive organisms of all.

Plants sense light, gravity, moisture, and chemicals.

Sniff
Sniff

They can even sense when they are being attacked.

When a plant is damaged by a hungry caterpillar, it can release chemicals that attract predators of the caterpillar.

What?

If the predator arrives in time, the plant might be saved—

SWOOP

—all because of the plant's senses.

Blow

MOVING

Animals have also adapted by developing specialized body parts that help them move across the land.

Mammals, birds, insects, and many reptiles and amphibians have legs with feet that allow them to move.

Feet are an adaptation for walking or running.

Most amphibians, mammals, and reptiles walk on four legs.

Insects have six legs, and spiders have eight.

Millipedes have hundreds of legs!

Some animals can crawl without legs and feet.

An earthworm crawls through the soil by alternately lengthening and shortening parts of its body.

Wings are an adaptation for flying.

Insects, bats, and birds have the ability to fly under their own power.

Bats are the only mammals with wings.

Batwings are made up mostly of skin stretched over long finger bones.

snatch

BzzT

Powerful muscles in the wings raise and lower them.

wap

wap

wap

Bird wings are covered with feathers that help them fly.

Movement for a plant can be difficult, since plants spend their whole life cycle in one spot.

When the soil of an environment lacks nutrients, the result can be harmful to plants in a few ways.

Lack of nutrients may cause changes in leaf color or leaf size, dead spots, reduced growth, and wilting.

Some plants have developed unusual adaptations to survive on soil low in nutrients.

Plop

Insect-eating plants get nutrients by trapping and digesting insects in their leaves.

Buzz

These plants break down the insects for nutrients, but also make their own food by photosynthesis.

Buzz

The Venus's-flytrap is a plant that has adapted to trapping insects in its leaves.

Snap

Ugh!

This plant grows in North American bogs where the soil has few nutrients, such as nitrogen or phosphorus.

Buzz

The insects provide these nutrients in the plant's diet.

BZZZ

Snap

After the plant has digested the insect, the trap opens again.

Burp

The leaf is now in position, waiting to capture the next insect.

PLANNING CHANGES

How both plants and animals meet their basic needs can affect other organisms in the environment.

If a herd of animals, or a species of plants, moves into a new environment, it can change the entire ecosystem in that area.

Humans, like you, are changing too.

Like all other organisms, you have basic needs that must be met to survive.

Farmers raise crop plants and farm animals for human use.

Farming is an adaptation that allows humans to concentrate less on finding food and more on other things...

chig

...like reading books!

Flip

Flip

However, entire ecosystems may be destroyed to make pasture land.

Some people believe that there is a way to create a balanced ecosystem, allowing all organisms to be successful.

This takes a lot of hard work and knowledge about the world around us.

But no matter what, we will always affect our environment, for better or worse.

So be sure that your decisions today will help to keep the ecosystem in good shape for generations to come!

TIMELINE

Ancient Greek philosopher Aristotle described many aspects of animal life and adaptations.

English naturalist Henry Bates described *mimicry* as a predator defense adaptation in insects.

335
B.C.

1861

1869

1927

German scientist Ernst Haeckel coins the term *ecology.*

English scientist Charles Elton described the circle of life.

1859

English scientist Charles Darwin described how species adapt to their environment by natural selection in his book, *On the Origin of Species.*

English scientist Arthur Tansley defined the concept of *ecosystem*.

1935

American biologist Raymond Lindeman described how energy and nutrients move through an ecosystem.

1942

English scientist James Lovelock described his *Gaia hypothesis* that suggests the Earth is a living organism adapted to function as a unified whole.

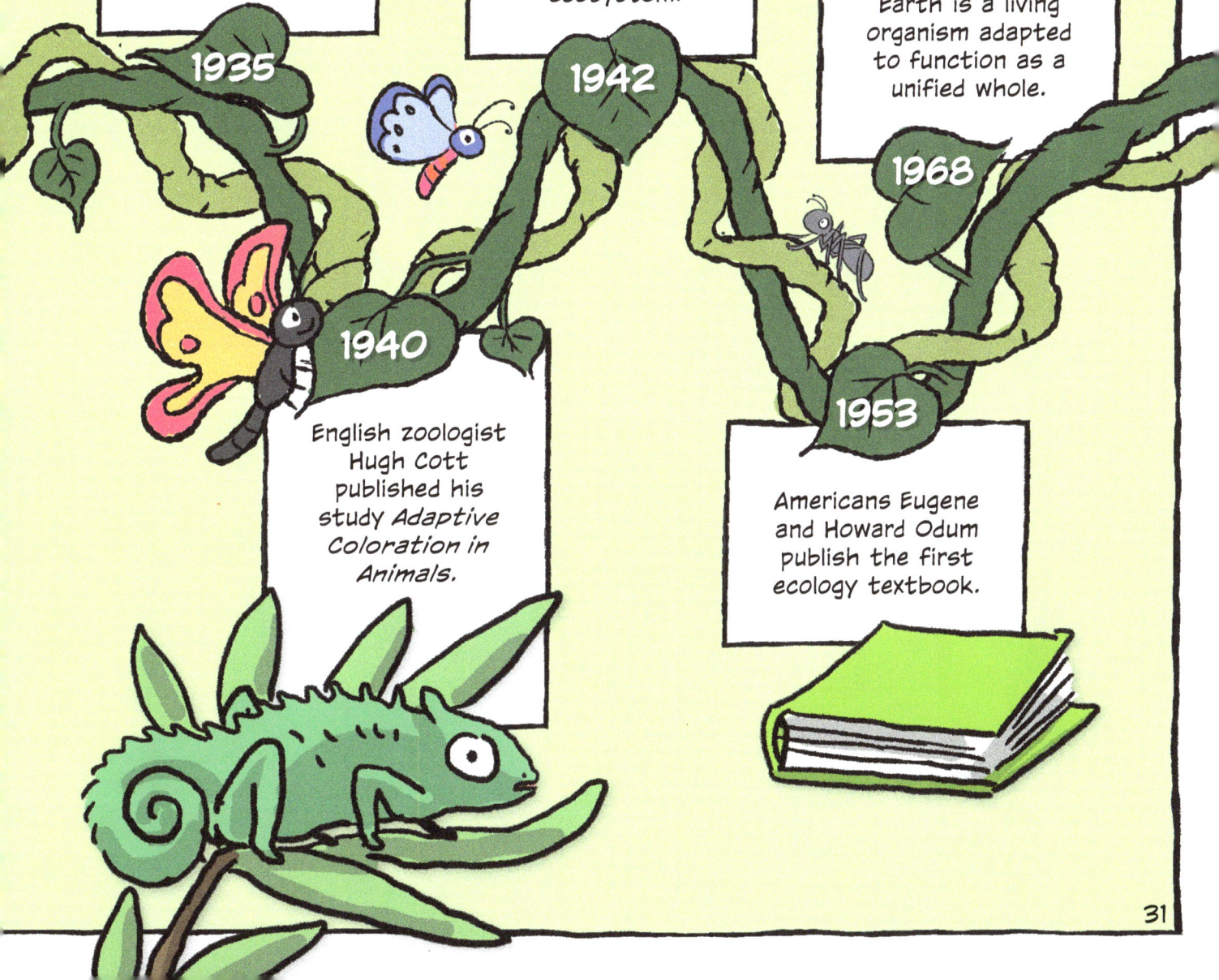

1968

1940

English zoologist Hugh Cott published his study *Adaptive Coloration in Animals*.

1953

Americans Eugene and Howard Odum publish the first ecology textbook.

WHO'S WHO: CHARLES DARWIN

Animals and plants are adapted to their surroundings to survive. Did you ever wonder just how those adaptations came about?

Let me tell you about a man called Charles Darwin.

Charles Darwin traveled around the world in 1835, observing all kinds of plants and animals in different habitats.

HMS BEAGLE

He found that some plants and animals had characteristics that allowed them to survive better.

Those individuals who survived went on to produce more offspring with the same characteristics.

Over time, the entire population possessed those characteristics. It is as if nature selected those who would survive! Only the ones who were adapted survived to reproduce.

You could say those that survived were the most fit. I call my theory "Survival of the fittest!"

Fact File

Name: Charles Darwin

Born: 1809 in Shrewsbury, England

Occupation: Naturalist

Claim to fame: Darwin described how species adapt to their environment by natural selection in his 1859 book, *On the Origin of Species.*

CAN YOU BELIEVE IT?!

When hibernating in winter, Alaskan wood frogs **may freeze solid** with no ill effects!

The tarsier can rotate its head 180 degrees and **look behind itself for enemies!**

Reindeer eyeballs turn blue in winter to help them see at lower light levels.

Some fish in the cold Southern Ocean have blood that acts **as anti-freeze!**

Cuttlefish have the most advanced color-changing adaptation of any animal. Their rapidly changing color patterns can be used as **camouflage** or for **communication.**

The deep sea giant isopod can go almost **five years without eating!**

The large ears of the fennec fox are not just for hearing. They also help this desert animal keep cool!

A kangaroo rat is so well adapted to its desert environment that it can **go its whole life without ever drinking water!** The animals get all the water they need from their food.

ACTIVITY: BE AN ECO-SCIENTIST WITH AN ECOSYSTEM CENSUS!

- String or thin rope, about 30 feet (10 meters)
- Paper notebook
- Pencil
- Magnifying glass
- Field guides

To study an ecosystem, scientists often examine a small portion of that ecosystem in detail. You can do the same in your own backyard or garden!

First, find an area in your yard or garden that interests you and lay out your string in a circle.

Choose a place that has a variety of plants and surfaces. This circle defines the ecosystem that you will study.

36

Then, study every detail of your ecosystem! Use field guides to help you identify rocks, plants, insects, and any other animals. Identify as many of the plants, animals, and rocks as you can.

Don't forget birds! Do you see any nests in the trees?

Record your findings in a notebook.

Take notes about everything you observe. Finally, make a detailed map of the ecosystem.

Write up your findings in a report. What kinds of adaptations do the plants and animals in your ecosystem have that allow them to survive there?

WORDS TO KNOW

adaptation any feature that helps a living thing survive in its environment.

algae a group of simple organisms that can make their own food. Algae contain chlorophyll but lack true stems, roots, or leaves.

characteristic special features and needs of an organism.

climate the long-term weather pattern in one location.

ecosystem all of the living and nonliving things in an area.

environment everything that is outside of a living thing.

generation a group of organisms that live during the same time period.

habitat the kind of place a living thing needs to live in to survive.

mammal a type of animal that has a backbone, grows hair, and feeds its young on the mother's milk.

natural selection the process in nature by which organisms with traits better suited for their environment survive, reproduce, and pass those traits to new generations.

nutrients substances that living things need to survive.

organism any living thing.

photosynthesis the process by which plants make their own food.

predator an animal that hunts and feeds on other animals.

prey an animal that is hunted by other animals for food.

reproduction the way living things make more of their own kind.

senses the way living things tell what is happening in the environment by hearing, sight, smell, taste, and touch.

species a group of closely related living things with many similarities.

trait a physical or behavioral characteristic of an organism.

variation the difference in characteristics within a group.

INDEX